For:
Carla
From
Sec

D0435556

POSEIDON PRESS . NEW YORK . LONDON
TORONTO . SYDNEY . TOKYO . SINGAPORE

Enough is Enough

by
Karen Finley

WEEKLY MEDITATIONS FOR
LIVING DYSFUNCTIONALLY

Poseidon Press

Simon & Schuster Building

Rockefeller Center

1230 Avenue of the Americas

New York, New York 10020

POSEIDON PRESS is a registered trademark of
Simon & Schuster Inc.

Designed by Barbara M. Bachman
Manufactured in the United States of America

10 9 8 7 6 5 4 3 2 1

Library of Congress Cataloging-in-Publication Data is available.

ISBN: 0-671-87182-X

TO DINO MORAITIS WITH
LOVE AND GRATITUDE

So what you're saying is You've never been so happy since you GAVE IN TO YOUR DYSFUNCTIONAL SELF + ENJOYED IT.

WHY LET GO WHEN YOU CAN CONTROL?

This Book Is
So Wrong On Many
Levels! Reverse Psychology
about how I precisely don't
want to be have control of
others, I don't even have
control of myself!

BEING IN CONTROL

Most people will advise you to let go and go with the flow. I ask, why? I advise you to be in control of as many people, situations and lives as possible. The most important reason to be in control is that it creates a much more interesting and complex life. And having a complex life is where it's at, especially if you are ever going to sell your life story. Being a control freak means you call the shots all the time.

Usually the people who tell us to stop controlling others are the ones who are in control of something but want to appear to be free, easy and open. Getting people not to be in control changes the power structure. It creates a bunch of selfless, uncomplaining goody-two shoes to take over and dominate. We are told to try and stop controlling others, but the reason we don't stop is because this is all we've got.

So stop the crap about trying to stop controlling others' lives. If all else fails, it's always good to pick a family member or friend whose behavior you want to control. You never will change their behavior, but it's your duty to try and control a family member. If you didn't, you wouldn't visit them at all. Then what would you do with your time? That goes for trying to control family gatherings—you know you won't, but you try to anyway, just for the hell of it. Controlling spouses is good too. We never do control them, but it sure is worth it to try.

It's important to get stressed out by having to be in control. Hopefully everyone will need you and your valuable time. Then you will deserve a vacation. Remember, being in control all the time makes vacations more important. The only control no-no is: Don't be a weekend control freak or vacation control freak.

MOTTO:

Why let go when you can control?

Blame = Assign responsibility for fault or wrong)

I BLAME MY MOM AND MY
GREAT GRANDFATHER — I
BLAME THE QUEST OF THE
HOLY GRAIL AND THE INVENTION
OF THE AUTOMOBILE. I BLAME
MY DAD AND
THE WAY HE
SPRINKLED
SUGAR. I
BLAME THE
WEATHER. I
BLAME televi-
SION FOR
EVERYTHING.
I BLAME ALL OF THESE
THINGS ON WHY I AM
SUCH A Profound INDIVIDUAL.

I play the "Blame game" A LOT!! This is what would fall into "Victim Mode"! I am not PERFECT. I need to own up to my shit! I need to see my mistakes, recognize them, own them, make amonds if possible, accept and move on! So and so hurt me! Dysfunctional Family! I got my feelings hurt by them. They don't like me, didn't invite me! I've blamed others my whole life, "Poor Me, Victim me, Help me. Feel Sorry for me." I can move forward, let go, move on, redirect my life, persevere! I DON'T HAVE TO BLAME OTHERS FOR MY SHIT! Work hard towards my goals!

BLAME

The best way to make our lives easier is to blame someone else for our mistakes. We know when we have made a mistake, so why the hell should we need to suffer the humiliation of accepting it publicly? It wastes time.

Blaming relatives is the best. Kids should blame parents for why they are so messed up, and parents should blame their kids for why they haven't done what they wanted with their lives. But then blaming transportation, the mail and the system also works to deflect the blame from yourself.

When you aren't to blame: *then* is the time to blame yourself. People will say, "No, no, you aren't to blame." Then cry and squeak a little and everyone will think you are so wonderful to accept blame for something you aren't responsible for.

TIP:

Blaming others for your mistakes is an effective way of getting out of a big mess.

Clothes NEVER looked SO GOOD ON HIM UNTIL HE BECAME
SELF INDULGENT

I am very self indulgent! It's all about me and nothing about others! I take advantage, use excuses, manipulate, lie! Wait, let me look up definition of self indulgent = doing or tending to do EXACTLY what one wants, especially when it involves pleasure and idleness! Well I'll say I self indulge in my addictions and I can learn to say no to myself, my disease and others! I don't have to feel guilty for saying NO! I like me staying at my christ night before xmas and Roberts wedding. So mom. I used to fix easters. I CAN SAY NO BUT NOT FOR SELFISH REASON

A QUICK WAY TO BE SELF-INDULGENT

Being self indulgent and totally selfish is a wonderful behavior to strive for. An easy way to quickly master this new attitude is to start saying no.

Many of you will say, "Hey, I don't have anything to be self-indulgent about without sounding arrogant and boring." A first step is to say no to requests of your time. Most people like to say yes and be trampled on for their giving natures. Then when they try and say no they feel guilty. Learn to say no with the pleasure of "I'm egotistical and I enjoy saying no." And for heaven's sake don't be a whiner when you say no. Say no with historical urgency.

If it is important, either they will call you back or you can call them back and say yes at a later time. In that case they will owe you something.

Remember, everything wraps around you. Everyone likes being around self-centered, pompous people. You can be certain self-indulgent people are always invited to parties, become celebrities and wear their clothes well.

Motto:

Being self-indulgent is an important accessory for anyone interested in social climbing.

I don't mean to BRAG-
BUT MY LIFE IS THE
GREATEST. I AM THE
GREATEST. MY WORK IS
INTELLIGENT IF NOT
GENIUS.
I'M
BORN
ON
JACKIE
GLEASON'S
Birthday.

It's OK for me to compliment myself! I mean, not to extreme but I can most certainly be proud of who I am, what I've done and how far I've come! law of attraction POSITIVE = POSITIVE

PUT IT OUT TO THE UNIVERSE!

SAY IT, SPEAK IT, SHOUT IT LIVE IT!

BRAGGING

In any matter, including religion, being humble doesn't work. People like to see other people FAIL. So when you say, "My work isn't that good," or "I don't look so hot," people listening will just not bother with you, for they want you to be an average, poor slob so that they can feel better than you.

That's why I say bragging is a good attitude. Any boring, menial job or situation will become better if you let everyone know that you are the greatest, the best at everything. What you usually do in your spare time should be much more interesting than what others do.

Say that you are the greatest at whatever career or interest that you have. Tilt your head back, hands in pockets, and stare into your brain and say in a sustained way—"My work is important, my life is sensational."

TIP:

Saying "I am great in bed" is definitely better than saying "I am okay in bed."

<u>SIGNS</u> OF GOOD TALKERS

 I KNOW I'VE HAD A GOOD TALKING WORKOUT WHEN MY JAW HURTs

 MY EAR USED TO HURT From being ON THE PHONE BUT NOW IT'S NICE AND CALLUSED

 FORGETS THE SUBJECT BUT KEEPS ON TALKING

 EVERYONE'S GONE BUT YOU'RE STILL TALKING

 VACATIONS ARE NOT FUN WHEN YOU DON'T HAVE A PHONE

TALK TOO MUCH

Stay away from those rigid, uncommunicative creatures who belch out, "You talk too much!" The best way to attack is to immediately make fun of them and then ignore them. That's right—don't talk to them at all. Let them be in their boring peace and quiet with no social life and no one to listen to.

Stop being embarrassed for talking on the phone all of the time or for having humongous phone bills. Phones were made to talk on. The only people who think that you are on the phone too much are people who don't have anyone to talk to.

When someone says, "You're still on the phone?" just reply, "Yes, I'm still on the phone, for I am lucky to have friends who enjoy speaking with me—not like you, who don't have any friends who call and want to talk to you. Your life must be pitiful if my friendships are of such great importance to you." Talking too much on the phone confirms to ourselves that we are popular and chatty.

Remember:
When you aren't talking, you are working, and who the hell wants to work?

FOR GUARANTEED WHINING
it's TONE FIRST—
VOLUME SECOND—
and content last.

WHINING

Whining is complaining about the future or upcoming events that you fear will give you something to complain about. It is always a good idea to whine about future social plans and to complain about the events before they happen. Whine about not having the clothes or the time, or whine about just not wanting to go to see some awful relative.

Whining is a useful technique for getting your own way, because people will just want to shut you up and will give you just about anything. The squeakiest wheel gets the oil. It is good to whine, because it makes you sound spoiled, and spoiled people are more interesting. Spoiled brats are always treated as special because they demand to be treated as special.

Extra Credit:

If whining doesn't work, sulk. If sulking doesn't work, cry. And if that doesn't work, cry and whine at the same time. That will ALWAYS work.

PROCRASTINATE

Always keep the phone off the hook to appear BUSY

PROCRASTINATE

Today is as good as any to give in to procrastination. The gentle art of procrastination is to enjoy putting off accomplishing something while people are waiting and calling. The pleasure is in having people wait for you. It is such a wonderful feeling to know people are waiting for us to finish, to start, to make a decision. Procrastinators will eventually accomplish the task. But time will pass and the deadline will be over and other work will just pile up.

Procrastination is very sexy, too. It's like putting off an orgasm with a lot of foreplay. And finally when you do it, it's such a relief.

Procrastination is healthy. You don't have to be depressed not to do something. You're just careful with your time.

Procrastination earns you respect. People will assume you are so busy and in demand that you can't possibly respond to them. When that happens, you will be more in demand and you will have more to procrastinate about.

MANTRA:
Maybe you want to put this one off till tomorrow?

FEELING BAD

Many of us try to stop feeling bad, but there are many great benefits to feeling bad. We usually keep the bad feelings to ourselves, and in order to benefit from this state of mind we must let it be known that we are feeling bad. Why? So that we can get someone we love to feel sorry for us.

Now, the easiest way to accomplish this is the sulk/pout look. You wait for someone to call, then speak slowly and painfully without hesitation or joy. When you talk to someone you love, have a frozen-stare expression and slightly greasy hair. When he asks, "What's wrong?" either say "Oh, nothing" with a depressed urgency or look out into space and admit, "I feel bad."

Once you learn to appreciate the enjoyment of feeling bad, you can try to get your friends to compliment you, give you cash, dinner invitations—all in the spirit of making YOU feel better. And you will feel better.

Sometimes special attention is what we need. Why fake feeling good when all you need is to enjoy feeling bad?

IMAGE:

When we go to the pound to pick out a pet, we always pick out the saddest-looking animal. Sad little puppy. Little neglected kitty.

Lie

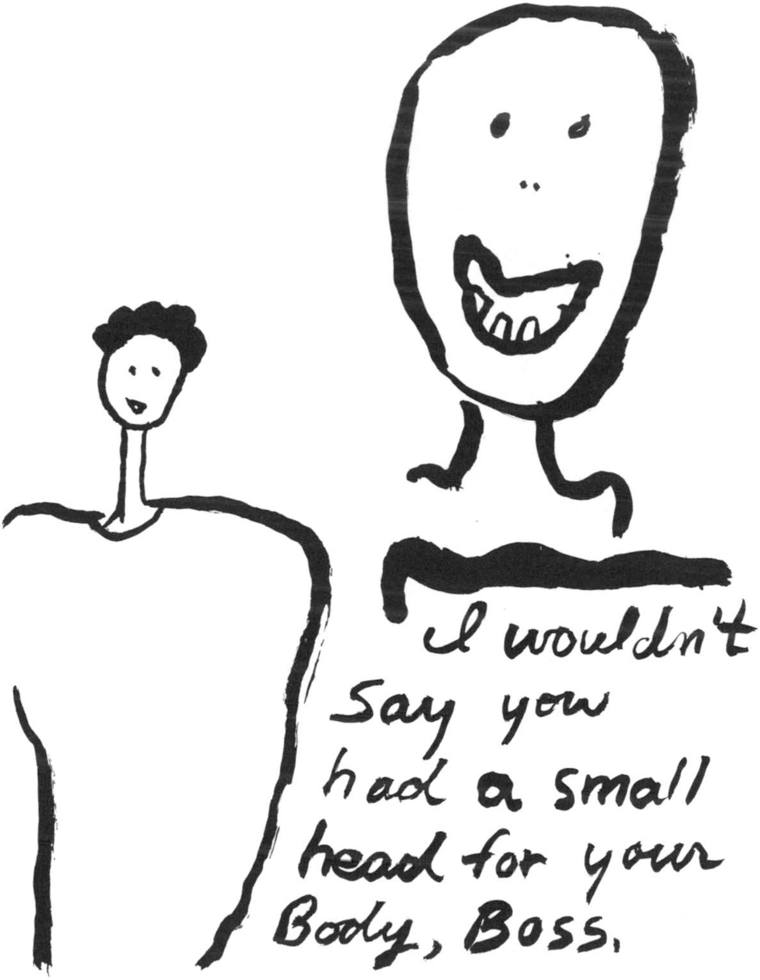

Telling the truth has the most disastrous consequences. What does telling the truth accomplish except peace of mind? What the hell does peace of mind do for you when you're trying to make a living? Really, what does telling the truth accomplish?

I say lie. Lie about your resume. Lie about where you have been. Lie about how good someone looks. Lie to take events to the extreme so that you are the good guy.

Lying is also the decent thing to do. Lie for yourself and the people you love. Movie stars, politicians, the media, our parents, all lie.

TIP:

If anyone ever questions you, just say, "Oh, I lied." Then laugh and say, "You believed me?"

I DON'T KNOW WHAT
THE HELL I'M DOING
BUT IF I DO IT
FAST, IN A FRANTIC
PACE, THEN I'll
get
AWAY
WITH IT.

BE HYPER

Don't stop your frantic pace. It's so much fun to always be in a whirlwind of busyness. It's a wonderful effect to have, always to be in a hurry, always speeding, never resting. We have a lot of stuff to do even if some of it is mundane—we need to get it done at an urgent pace.

So when you are told to relax or take it easy, just think to yourself, "No, I don't have time for you and I despise slow movers." If you want to say it to their faces—good for you.

It's exciting to move quickly, doing a lot. We get our hearts racing and it's fun living the life of a roller-coaster bitch on wheels.

MANTRA:
Everyone hates a slow driver.

GOING CRAZY

YES, WE ARE IN
FOR SOME ART—
She's GONE OFF
AGAIN

ACTING CRAZY

Acting crazy is a wonderful asset for living a romantic, artistic life. Going crazy makes any relationship wild with passion and adds some spice to the routine of experience. After you go crazy, you can pick up the pieces. It's a comfortable cycle that artists have used for centuries.

Just appreciate your craziness and get some mileage out of it, some acknowledgment, some prestige. Being seen as a little bit off creates mystery and excitement. It is important always to have your creative talents or love interest involved with you acting crazy. The best love is passionate, crazy, lustful lovemaking.

Whether you are a writer, a painter or a person who just needs amusement, acting crazy is to be recommended. My favorite artists are the ones perceived as crazy by society— van Gogh, Sylvia Plath, Marilyn Monroe, to name only a few.

HINT:

It is nonproductive to act crazy about taking out the garbage, menus and politics.

HA HA HA I HAVEN'T HAD SO MUCH FUN IN YEARS. WHO CAN WE MAKE FUN OF NEXT?

MAKE FUN OF SOMEONE TODAY

Making fun of people is an enjoyable pastime to develop alone or with others. It relieves a lot of stress and it certainly is nonviolent. I suggest you make fun of your employers, people who are snotty to you and people whom you envy.

The most satisfying way to make fun of someone is to make fun of that person while he is in the same room, without him knowing. Parties, gallery openings, community events are all good places. Of course, to his face you are cordial. You'd be happy to say these things to his face but you are civilized so you can't, and making fun of him is the next best thing.

It someone makes your life miserable, make every effort to make fun of him in social situations. Forget about that crap of "Don't talk behind someone's back" or "If you can't say something nice, don't say it at all." That person has probably been mean to you AND DESERVES EVERY MINUTE OF PRIVATE HUMILIATION YOU GIVE.

IMAGE:
The laughter from making fun of someone is a beautiful song.

You're FIRED
AND IN 2 YEARS EVERYThing WILL BE GONE- AND YOU'LL have TO WORK FOR ME!

CURSE

CURSES

As soon as someone does something horrible to you, such as fire you, steal your lover or ruin your life, put a curse on her. Of course, you should do this in private and don't tell people what you are planning to do. You merely wish her business to go under or for her relationship to utterly fail. Then wait.

When her business, finances, or relationship goes under, just say in public, "Oh, I'm sorry." You could also tell people, "I put a curse on her a while ago," so that they will be wary of you. Then celebrate when the person who destroyed you suffers. Because now she knows how it feels.

REMEMBER:

It feels good to see people you hate suffer.

REVENGE
ROACH IN THE FOOD!

your opening
IS RUINED —
I FEEL GOOD.

REVENGE

To be a balanced person, it helps to know the gentle art of revenge. Forget about letting go. Use your anger as fuel for creative energy or legal action. Getting even is a wonderful way to spend your time and energy.

You can create artworks that publicly humiliate those who deserve it. Make them the central characters in a book, painting, lectures or jokes. When you have writer's block, make a list of those who were cruel to you and get back at them later in your creative life. Make art out of all the mean things they did to you and try to make some money out of the revenge while you are at it. Or get back at them through legal processes—IRS, taxes, lawsuits. Or just constantly bad-mouth them.

TIP:
The results of revenge keep one looking youthful and perky.

JERKS, MOVE OUT OF THE WAY!
Oh, GOOD AN ASSHOLE IN THE BIG CITY!
CAN'T WAIT TO TELL THEM BACK HOME! A REAL LIVE ASSHOLE

BEING AN ASSHOLE

Being an asshole is a delightful way to behave with strangers. You don't say thank you. You are snide. You cut off slow drivers. You don't return phone calls. You always keep your answering machine on. You are a generally rude person. That means being rude to tourists, and when you are a tourist you are a total asshole too.

Being an asshole is beneficial because you can generally be rude to strangers and not take things out on your real friends. It is an etiquette that provides relief from always being courteous and thinking about others' feelings.

Taking a few minutes out of your day to be an asshole to strangers will provide the necessary relief. An asshole can make driving a good time by just honking for the hell of it. Everyone expects assholes in a city. The people who live in cities relish the asshole image, which keeps everyone at a distance, and small-town folk like seeing assholes in a city, for then they can convince themselves that it is better to live in their boring hometown.

It is difficult to be an asshole if you live in a small town because you are expected to be sweet and quaint, but you can get back at tourists who come to your town for events such as craft fairs. Craft fairs are a wonderful place to be an asshole by saying loud ugly remarks about the ugly goods people are trying to sell.

REMEMBER:
Being an asshole is quite a civilized tradition.

Always
Be A Bitch
whenever
possible

BEING A BITCH

Being a bitch is when you can't be an asshole because you need to be mean to the people you *know*. You need to be mean because everything else is boring or bullshit and the people you are around are so stupid and proper that the only way to act is to be a bitch.

It's important to let people know that you are in pain but you control that pain. Perhaps they don't have the capacity for anything except the usual garbage normalcy and you are different because you are a bitch.

A bitch must dress well. You can't be a bitch and a lousy dresser. You must look good and prefer solids.

When bitching, don't look people in the eye. They don't deserve it. Say everything to the side with your head tilted up with authority, disdain and drama. A great bitch is someone who can say a cruel remark and everyone in the room is amused because for a few minutes their lives are not so awfully boring. The bitch is the performer.

It is very good to learn to be a bitch, because then we have personality, then we have fun, then we have friends who look up to us because we are a bitch.

TIP:

Be a bitch whenever possible. You always look better when acting like a bitch.

I don't look at it that
I have a spending problem
I look at it
that I'm
a
good
American

SHOPPING

Consuming is an American religion, so buy, buy, buy. The reason we buy so much is that we've got to have something to show for our hard day's work. Shopping is the great American pastime.

The responsibility of being an American brings with it the patriotic duty to consume. So when that cheap, stingy person gives you that look and says, "You bought what?" "You spent your savings on that?" "You really needed that?" just look him straight in the face and say, "Yes, I bought that because it gives my life pleasure, not like you who live your life for a boring, pathetic future that will never be. You are so cheap you let the sponge fall apart before you buy a new one. You are a disgusting example of an American."

Motto:

Just tell them that you are helping the economy.

I HATE YOUR GUTS!
You're AN HONEST PERSON. I like YOUR STYLE.
HATE

HATE

Feeling hate toward an individual or a society is very energizing. If you can hate something, then you can love something. Everyone likes to say it is bad to live with hate in our hearts. Why? If someone is mean to you and hurts you, then it is right and proper to hate that person.

Everyone teaches us that the hate feeling is an awful feeling to have. I disagree. We should admit our hate, recognize the feeling. And when we have the opportunity, we should vocalize the sentiment. Begin by saying the words of hate slowly. Then speed up till the words come out with venomous spittle, with a thrill that will chill whoever hears you and make them understand that you mean what you say. Always be passionate, with strong-feeling words. You aren't talking about milk.

If you want to stop being a spineless worm, recognize and vocalize your hate today.

Example:

I hate people who use leaf blowers and I take every opportunity to tell them I hate their activity.

ACTING LIKE YOUR PARENTS

DOESN'T EVERYONE REUSE TOOTHPICKS?

ACTING LIKE YOUR PARENTS

We all catch ourselves acting like our parents. Having annoying habits like your parents' can be endearing to the one you love. It is a good idea to take your intimate other to meet your parents and view their disgusting, annoying habits for himself. You want your intimate other to see your parents' offensive presentations of themselves so he has the opportunity to witness how truly messed up you deserve to be.

Once your lover sees how messed up your parents are, your lover will find that your endearing habits (like farting while walking to the fridge, slurping and licking the coffee cup, making smacking sounds with your teeth or needing to read an entire encyclopedia to make a B.M.) are gross but basically harmless.

HINT:

Acting like your parents is a good test for tolerance in your mate.

EMBRACE THE PROBLEMS OF OTHERS

If your life is average and healthy and therefore you are lonely and feeling like you don't fit in, maybe what you need to do is embrace other people's problems. Get involved in other people's problems as if they were your own. Try reinforcing their weaknesses. Recognize these traits as a vital part of their life force and you will be guaranteed relationships of high-volume dysfunctional dynamics that will endure your entire lifetime.

You won't feel alone anymore when you're getting calls at three A.M. from crying, out-of-control souls who need to dump their problems on you. You'll have plenty to do when your day is filled up with endless visits to people who want your attention while they describe how their lives are going down the toilet.

Motto:
Feeling needed makes us feel wanted and loved and that is what's important.

Personal Melodrama

I make taking out the
garbage into A
GREEK Tragedy

PERSONAL MELODRAMA

No matter how well or how bad life is going, one should always do it with flair. This means creating personal melodrama in everyday life. Buying a pot holder should be like a scene from the Bible. Taking out the garbage, like an act from your favorite episode of *Mission: Impossible*. Every banal, inane part of your life should have an outfit, an attitude, be a dramatic part of your characterization for the day.

Live each moment like a scene from a Tennessee Williams play. Everything should be too much or too little. It is good to keep in touch with those who attract melodrama, so you can play the savior or victim. Create scenes. When you don't get what you want, make it an Oscar-winning performance. Yes, people will be embarrassed, but they will remember you.

REMEMBER:

Creating personal melodrama out of everyday living makes our lives interesting even when they aren't.

LET'S BE JEALOUS
MORE OFTEN!

JEALOUSY

I think it is stupid when people hand us this pathetic myth that it is not good to feel jealous or act jealous. You bet I'm going to be jealous when someone else gets what I deserve. Or when the person I love shows more attention to someone other than me.

The best thing to do for jealousy within a relationship is at least to try to have some great sex, or wait a few days, not letting up on the jealousy bit, and then have some great sex.

When you are jealous of someone for having something you don't, sometimes you just have to wait for them to become a has-been.

REMEMBER:

Jealousy can lead to passionate lovemaking.

BAD HABITS

When people tell you to stop biting your nails or chewing on a pencil, just look them straight in the eye and say, "You are lucky this is my bad habit. I could be a crack addict. I could be a compulsive gambler. So don't tell me to stop twiddling my thumbs." That will shake them up and get them to mind their own business.

If they stare at you while you are rocking your leg in a spastic movement and they ask you to stop it, say, "Yeah, I'm nervous a little, but I go to work. I make a living." Name all of their bad habits and then yell them out in public. That will get them to shut up, and that takes care of that problem.

Remember:
Your bad habit might be the good habit of someone else.

I'm not hysterical
I'm just letting
my inner child out

BLAME YOUR INNER CHILD

It is always a good idea to exploit current self-help philosophies. That is why I strongly encourage you to blame your inner child for just about everything you do. When you have been crabby, sulky, manipulative or just plain impossible to live with, announce that you were letting your inner child out. Explain your reckless behavior as something that was spiritually healthy for you.

When you've just screamed at your boss—blame your inner child. When you've just been caught going ninety m.p.h.—blame your inner child. When you've just polished off two boxes of Ring Dings—blame your inner child.

TIP:

Don't bother doing this alone. This is the type of behavior that needs a public.

Forget the easy way out.
Keep it complicated. And
you'll enjoy the complications
for years.

KEEP IT SIMPLY COMPLICATED

It's to your advantage to complicate your life. In this way you will appear to be doing so much in this world and it will seem that so much is happening to you. Make simple everyday events that happen to everyone into psychodrama. Take common fates that pass uneventfully through the lives of most people and turn them into grueling, heart-wrenching, soul-searching intrigues that last till the next trauma occurs.

Getting over the low hurdles in life is easy. It's getting over the high hurdles that attracts people's attention. A simple life is boring. Every complicated setback should be appreciated because overcoming it makes the triumph look that much greater.

Hint:
A complicated life has so many opportunities.

Don't look at it as
complaining ~
Look at it
as
trying
to
get
to
know
me
better

COMPLAINING

When there isn't much to complain about in your life and you need to relieve a little stress, just complain about how you were treated in some situation several years ago. Don't complain about things that are important in your life now; don't get personal. This way no one can come up with a perfect solution to resolve the horrible scenario that you have just enjoyed setting up.

It is important to find good places in which to complain. It is very satisfying to complain in a restaurant. Complain about the food, the lighting, the noise, the fact that the pasta spoon is a teaspoon, the fact that they don't serve balsamic vinegar or that the red wine is chilled.

TIP:

If you are a big complainer, remember when in your favorite restaurant to doubly tip your server or suffer the consequences.

A sense of self worth with every ignored phone call.

RRRRING RRRING

IGNORING

When you feel worthless and like a nobody, it's time to ignore people. Why should you have to suffer all alone? Try to make others feel worthless too. Ignoring others can be done in subtle ways—not answering phone calls, not hearing someone call out your name, walking past someone you know without acknowledging him. These are all ways of winning back your self-confidence.

If you are in a work situation where everyone eats together, eat alone; go home alone every night and your aloofness will intrigue everyone. They will start asking you about yourself and shortly you will begin to feel better.

REMEMBER:
Ignoring others leads to greater self-esteem.

NO ONE WILL
ASK YOU STUPID
QUESTIONS WHEN
YOU ARE JUST
PLAIN MEAN

JUST PLAIN MEAN

Being just plain mean means that you try to be equally mean to everyone for no particular reason. Offer no thank-you's or pardon-me's but rather grunts and sighs as if everyone is in your way. The strategy is to make everyone stay out of your way because your life is more relevant than theirs and then they won't waste your time with their casual, determined niceties, their small talk and their cheerfulness. All cheerful talk or positive attitudes by strangers should be responded to with a groan or the phrase "I really don't care" or with a stare, clenched teeth, curled lip or a growl—then look in the other direction. That will show them not to interfere with your mean old self.

REMEMBER:

People stay away from old mean dogs; nice dogs always get stuck doing stupid dog tricks.

GET ME OUT OF HERE! I hate Being in a Room with contented adults.
ESCAPE NOW

ESCAPE

As soon as you attend one of those boring, obligatory social events and your blood boils and your teeth clench and you get the worst headache of your life, leave. Just get the hell out of there. Never endure it. The feeling of escape will be wonderful.

Some people like a sauna, a massage or a cold shower, but give me the benefits of leaving, escaping: the heightened pulse rate, the sweaty palms and then, when you are finally out, the thrill of freedom. Leaving without telling a soul is such an extreme pleasure.

Don't try to cover up, saying that you have diarrhea or hot flashes or vertigo. Just say to the other guests, "I've got to get the hell out of here." Hopefully you will never be invited back to these damn gatherings again.

FACT:

Even though you try to lose contact with these people, they will continue to send you holiday and birthday greetings for years.

I KNOW I SHOULD SHARPEN THIS PENCIL _NOW_ — BUT I'D RATHER THINK ABOUT THE _PAST_ — WHEN I DIDN'T HAVE A PENCIL — OR THE _FUTURE_ WHEN THIS PENCIL WILL BE SHARPENED DOWN TO NOTHING.

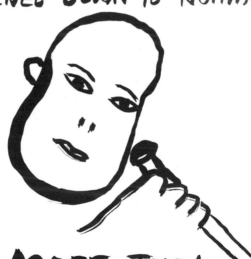

TAKE MORE THAN ONE DAY AT A TIME

TAKING MORE THAN ONE DAY AT A TIME

Living for today may seem like a simple solution to life's problems, but it is more complicated than it looks. You have to deal with the ups and downs of each day and actually solve your problems.

It is beneficial to worry about what is going to happen next week and to go over and over in your mind incidents that occurred in the past. Why? Because then you don't have to deal with the problems that are facing you now, in the present, and everyone knows that now will pass and you can worry about it later, in the future.

Everyone has been living this way for years. Don't mess it up.

REMEMBER:

"Be here now" is for people with no life.

I know why. It's because
the lake is fed by an UNDERGROUND
spring that was a feeding
ground for a now extinct form
of PERCH. I know why - Because
the ASPHALT is the last to freeze.
I know WHY, the gray squirrel and
blue jay fight. I know why -
Because the fashion industry
dictated the women's magazines.
I know why - Sufism has
something   I
to do   know.
with
telling
a good
story.

KNOW-IT-ALLS

Have you ever been with a group of people where everyone understood intimidating, complex subjects and you felt like a bumbling idiot? You probably kept quiet and nodded your head and tried to smile intelligently, but baby, that ain't going to get you anything but neck pains from nodding your head like a chicken.

Be a know-it-all. It's easy. Actually, all the people who are acting like they know everything are probably merely know-it-alls.

Know-it-alls are instant experts on any subject no matter how arcane or specialized. They just declare some facts or some personal story in regard to the topic, and if they don't have any knowledge of the subject, they just make it up.

HINT:

Making up knowledge is really all that fiction writers do. So making the whole damn thing up is what being creative is all about.

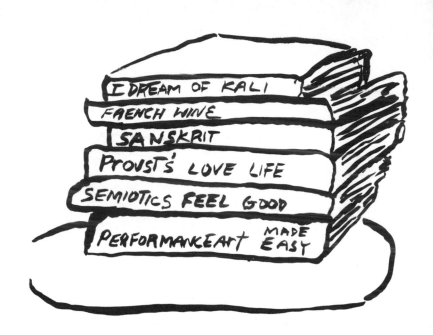

I DREAM OF KALI

FRENCH WINE

SANSKRIT

PROUST'S LOVE LIFE

SEMIOTICS FEEL GOOD

PERFORMANCE Art MADE EASY

example of how to
arrange books to
appear smart, hip & cool

BOOKS ON DISPLAY

Books aren't only for reading. They are also a vital decorative embellishment or prop that can quickly guide houseguests into thinking that their host is bright and thoughtful. To accomplish this, you should buy books on self-help, dreams, City Lights authors, fiction, art and poetry, and scatter them around the house. Make sure to buy them at a used-book store because the book will appear to have been read.

It's good to have a pile by your bed—include one on history, one on politics and two trashy novels or biographies. In the bathroom leave a book by anyone who committed suicide. Obscure books on such topics as mosaics in Ravenna, ant farms, UFOs and contemplative religious life should be put in the living room.

If anyone picks out a book and asks you if you have read it, say, "I'm having a difficult time getting through it."

HINT:

For that extra touch of realism, make sure there are a few books with bookmarks left opened.

I can't wait to
disclose this intimate
moment
in
group.

LYING ABOUT THERAPY

Whether you go to therapy or not, tell everyone that you see a therapist and that you've been going for years. It comes in handy when you don't have anything planned and you need to get out of doing something. Just say, "Oh, sorry, I have to go to group," or "I'll talk to my therapist about it. You mean you don't go?"

It's very important to let people assume that you go for psychological help, because that makes you a more complex personality. It adds a sense of mystery to an otherwise dull and boring life. People will always wonder, "Hmmm, I wonder why she has to go to a shrink?"

Think of mentioning your therapy sessions in the same way you talk about professional sports. Talk about your therapist with as much enthusiasm as you would talk about a new recipe in *The New York Times*.

TIP:
Casually referring to your therapist makes you appear cool and is especially effective when wearing a turtleneck and designer glasses.

GRANDPA WAS AN ELEVATOR OPERATOR
CHANGE TO **MAGICIAN**

GRANDMA WAS JUST A NICE LADY
CHANGE TO - **CLAIRVOYANT**

DAD ~~WAS A~~ LIKED FOOTBALL
CHANGE TO - **HIGH STAKE GAMBLER**

MOM LIKED GARDENING
CHANGE TO -
PRACTICED **HOMEOPATHIC HEALING**
and FBI HAS A FILE ON HER

TRY IT - IT WORKS

REINVENT YOUR FAMILY

REINVENT YOUR FAMILY

One of life's sadder bequests is coming from a family that is average. It follows that you, being born of average stock, are probably average too. It is important then to boost, or some would say reinvent, your genealogy.

Make up some event of major historical importance or some important crisis that has happened to you and your family. You can include aunts and uncles, cousins and neighbors, too. Messy divorces, being written out of wills, and family members going through rehab are all accepted topics. A good birth-trauma story is also good for attention.

REMEMBER:

It is such a happy day when a listener says, "Boy, you sure come from a crazy family."

KU- BEE
coobie
cool bee

In the Art world
Would you say it's
historically significant,
or that you don't get it?

OBSCURE ART EVENTS

It is important to attend some obscure artistic exhibition or event where the artist is so distant, the creator/performer so arcane, that even having three Ph.D.s will not help you understand it any better.

The main reason to go is so that you will be able to use vocabulary that you have been hearing and reading but don't quite understand. You will be able to use academic words or hip art-words like "juxtapose," "contextualize," "appropriate" and "deconstructionist" when commenting on art.

Make sure to let everyone know that you have attended such an event, and if you didn't understand it, never say that it was "interesting" or "neat." Say either "I understand it historically" or "I can appreciate its minimalness."

REMEMBER:

Attending an obscure, out-of-the-way cultural experience qualifies one for the title of trendsetter.

Arrive Late

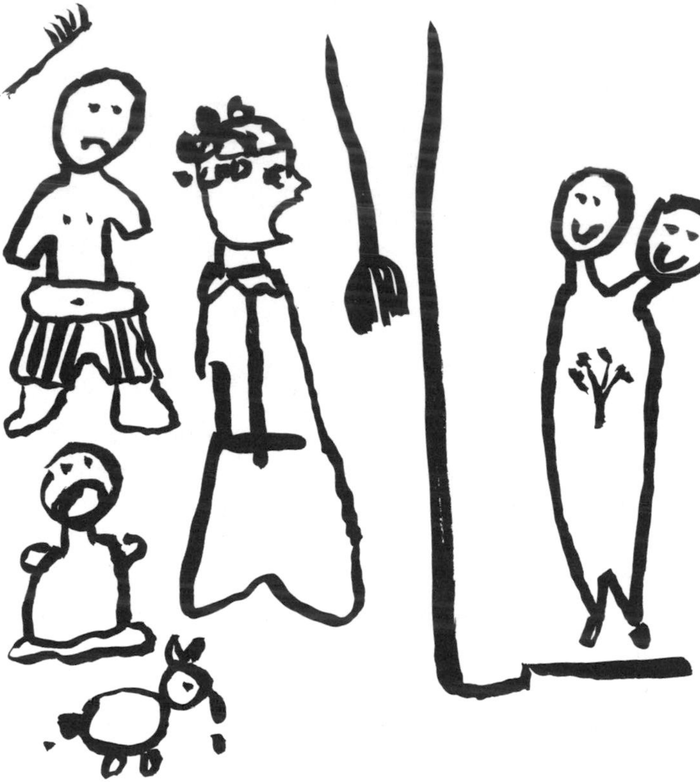

Oh No, They're on time!

ARRIVE LATE

People who arrive late are appreciated because most decent, hardworking people are never ready to expect you to be on time. This is especially true when going to someone's home for dinner. Please don't arrive exactly on the button. It is rude. Hosts enjoy waiting for their guests and wondering, "Where are they?" Most people hate guests who arrive early for parties. That can be said for meetings, jobs, etc. There is nothing worse than an eager beaver excited to do some crummy job. WHY? Because a punctual person makes everyone else look stupid and then everyone else will team up against you.

Arriving late declares your rudeness factor from the beginning. It lays the groundwork for sophistication and intelligence. Now, I'm not talking about arriving hours late, as each situation has its allowable span of tardiness. Usually it is best to allow that phrase "Where are they?" to pass, and then arrive—calm and in control. The person expecting you wants you to be there and you are there and everything falls in place.

TIP:

When you arrive late, don't wear too much cologne or look like you just washed your hair.

HOW TO DEAL WITH LOSERS

For every winner in this world there is at least one loser. How lucky you are to have some pathetic creep wanting to be your friend. True losers will never accept no for an answer; they will corner you whenever they see you and think that they are on your best-friend list. When a loser approaches, certain lines like "I've got to get going" or "I forgot your name" actually get a loser even more excited and more determined to be your friend.

We need losers, because no social event is truly a success without a few of these lost souls. When talking with friends and approached by a loser, you should say, "Excuse me, but I'm in deep conversation here," and the loser walks away and you can go back to talking about how the hostess's panty hose is falling down. Then you can say, "Tsk, tsk. He/she is such a loser." Then you feel like you are in the company of winners. Don't feel bad for losers, for they enjoy their role.

TIP:

We bond with other winners by expressing mutual contempt for losers.

MAKE A SCENE IN PUBLIC

Don't just hold in your rage when the florist you've patron-ized for years won't give you change for the bus. Don't just let it go when an advertised item on sale is not in stock. Don't just stand there when your cashier is slow, stupid, or cracks gum in an annoying fashion. Make a scene in public. It's therapeutic.

Make humiliating, sarcastic remarks like "I can see why you're working at such a crappy job. It doesn't take much brains or class" or "You're the reason why this country is such a mess—you don't know how to add, you're a slob and you have no work ethic."

You should never repress your feelings and think of yourself as a loser who deserves to be treated poorly again. Whenever you feel the least bit slighted, start screaming or yelling some-thing sarcastic and watch the response you'll get.

EXTRA CREDIT:

For maximum effect when making a public scene in a store, try to involve as many other customers in your tantrum as possible.

I'M SORRY I ASKED YOU TO SMILE

FORGOING PLEASANTRIES

When meeting strangers, it is customary in our society to be pleasant. There are formalities, especially when one is shopping, that are considered mandatory. Smiling for no reason and answering stupid, mundane questions are two of life's more annoying tasks.

Whenever people ask you to smile, it is a good time to release all your frustrations. Just look at them with a grimace and say, "I don't want to smile." Since these people are sadists, they will then say, "But you look so much prettier/more handsome when you smile," and you should reply, "Well, I certainly don't want to disappoint your pathetic expectations," and then make an exaggerated smile-monster-face.

When confronted with some stranger working in a service industry, such as a shoe salesman who eagerly inquires "How are you?" as you enter the store, it is time to teach him to stop lying. Look at him and say, "Do you really care how I am? Well, I'll let you know. I'm depressed, in debt, I just lost my apartment and my pet died. I came in to buy a pair of slippers for my dying grandfather, but now I'm not in the mood."

TIP:
If you live in New York City, you probably don't need to read this one.

the longer I stay
in my bad mood
the easier for me
to maintain the
title   DIFFICULT

BEING DIFFICULT

When you are lucky enough to acquire a bad mood, try to stay in it as long as possible. Being in a bad mood is to be considered a higher state of consciousness. You are questioning the crap in this world. By being in a bad mood, you demonstrate to others your fine, keen sensitivities, your idealism in not being satisfied with the way things are.

We, as a culture, are really only interested in people who are in bad moods—celebrities, writers, musicians, artists and sports figures have drawn much attention to themselves and their art with their bad moods and tantrums.

Remember:

In reality, people in good moods get on our nerves. No one likes to hang around with a good-mood person who is happy all the time, and, at all costs, avoid anyone with the nickname Chipper.

Adventures in KARMA

WHEN JEFF WAS 3 HIS MOST FUN WAS STEPPING ON ANTS UNTIL...

HE WAS TOLD ABOUT KARMA AND THAT SOMEDAY SOMETHING WOULD STEP ON HIM. THERE WENT THAT FUN.

Rejecting Karma

REJECTING KARMA

Doesn't it make you gag when you do something minor in regard to the total cosmos such as call in sick to work or double-park your car and someone says to you, "You better watch out for your karma." Just look at him and say, "I hate karma. Karma was invented so that the poor and miserable would accept their condition without rebelling."

Karma only comes in handy when someone has fired you, takes your parking space or takes your clothes out of the dryer at the laundromat. In the world we live in, it is getting too risky to yell at someone. You may get shot. So then and only then can you call on karma.

TIP:

Never name a child Karma, not even as a middle name. Pets don't like it either.

I'd know that face anywhere — A HAPPY HEART BECAUSE HE NEVER FULFILLED HIS DREAMS

THE VALUE OF UNFULFILLED DREAMS

I say having dreams and staying in that dream state is euphoric. It's a lot of work to get off your butt and make something of yourself. It's a lot more fun to dream.

If someone cracks down on you for never realizing your dreams, just look at her and say pathetically, "Am I hurting anyone by dreaming?" Then try to attack her with her own accomplishments, like, "I wasn't built for bungee jumping, like you," or "I never had EST training, like you did."

If that doesn't work, ask her to lend you some money to pursue your dream. That'll shut her up.

TIP:
Wear a T-shirt that says, WHEN DREAMS COME TRUE, THEY STOP BEING DREAMS.

the only way I'm
going to feel better is
by buying something I'll
never use or wear

BUYING THINGS THAT YOU DON'T NEED

The easiest way to feel luxurious, with no cares in the world, is to buy things that you don't need. This is an important process in life, because you really feel that you would achieve something if only you had the right tools, the right accessories. What is even better is to buy something that you will never even use, such as ice-fishing equipment or a yogurt maker or a bottle cutter to make glasses for Christmas presents until you realize that they are stupid gifts.

Buying something that in your wildest imagination you know you will never use and trying to convince yourself that you need it has some wonderful beneficial effects that modern science cannot explain. The reason is that when you do pass up something to buy, you are sure to desperately need the item the next day. So the best way to avoid that situation of needing size $6^1/_2$ turquoise velvet shoes, or a telephone in the style of Cinderella's pumpkin carriage, and having passed up the opportunity to acquire it the day before, is to purchase it when you see it. Buy that shower curtain that changes color with the water temperature. Buy a picnic table and barbecue even though you don't have a yard.

REMEMBER:
Any association with fondue sets enables us to participate in this ancient tradition.

WHAT'S NEEDED

GOOD DEPRESSED MOOD, TV, CABLE REMOTE CONTROL, ASSORTMENT OF TAKEOUT MENUS, PHONE, MONEY FOR DELIVERY OF PIZZA + CHINESE FOOD, TV GUIDE, TRASHY READING, FAVORITE PAJAMAS AND ROBE

STAY IN BED ALL DAY

STAY IN BED ALL DAY

When you feel down and out and depressed, instead of fighting it, stay in bed all day. It is wonderful to be in bed and do nothing. Keep the TV on, stay in your pajamas all day, eat takeout food from the cartons and wallow in your misery.

Then make sure to tell people that you are in bed for the day. While in this condition call people from bed, and when they ask what you are doing, say in a husky, sexy, not-woken-up voice, "I'm still in bed." Those words will create a visual image of you as Andy Warhol calling Edie Sedgwick or Marilyn Monroe calling Bobby Kennedy or Truman Capote calling Jackie O. How very talented and on-the-scene you are.

TIP:
Make sure that you still brush your teeth even if you're staying in bed all day.

DEAR, DON'T EVER SAY
YOU FORGOT
show some manners AND
MAKE AN EXCUSE!

MAKE AN EXCUSE

If there is something that you don't want to do, don't waste your time trying to confront the source of your apprehension, or spend time trying to figure out why you can't deal with doing something—simply make up an excuse and be done with it.

Excuses are an accepted way of getting out of something that you don't like. It is a good idea to have a stockpile of all-purpose excuses ready for any occasion. Fine examples of excuses are: I have a bad back, I have a weak stomach, My parents are in town, I won't be in town. I'm sure we can all think of situations in which these excuses could be put to good use. If you get caught, just say, "It's funny how things worked out, but my plans changed."

REMEMBER:
It is perfectly all right to invent excuses, because excuses are false in the first place.

REAL STORY

THEY WERE MAKING A SANDWICH
AND THEY <u>ALMOST</u> DROPPED IT.

 He's BORING

WITH THE HELP OF EXAGGERATION...

THEY WERE MAKING A SANDWICH
AND IT DROPPED **ON** THE FLOOR.
AND THEY SERVED IT—
THERE WAS ALL
THIS HAIR + CRUD
ON IT.

THIS GUY KNOWS
HOW TO TELL A STORY—

MORE FRIENDS—
MUCH MORE EXCITING LIFE

EXAGGERATE!

EXAGGERATE

There is nothing worse than some bore who always has to tell a story exactly the way it happened. No one cares. People want to be amused by a good story. Exaggerate! Exaggerating makes all stories better. Exaggerators aren't liars, they're just entertaining personalities.

And always stay away from video cameras and people who film or tape every event and family gathering. Video cameras are the curse of the exaggerator. No one can embellish a story when confronted with the facts right in front of her on someone's TV. The best stories are always the ones that we exaggerate. A good exaggerator will never be considered a bore.

TIP:
Exaggerating makes our lives more creative and inventive without much money.

AS SOON AS YOU TOLD ME IT WASN'T GOOD FOR ME— IT TASTED SO MUCH BETTER

GUILT MAKES LIFE MORE PLEASURABLE

GUILT

Guilt is the most important emotion of all. Without it no one would feel obligated to do anything. There is so much focus on trying to get people not to feel guilt. Normal people do feel guilt. People who don't feel guilt are called sociopaths.

What we are addressing here is good old-fashioned guilt that makes sex, passion, food, lust, overspending—just about anything—much more pleasurable. Normal and healthy people are ones who have some guilt about things like sex and eating in the middle of the night. Everything seems a little better when accompanied by guilt. When you feel it, just admit it to yourself and get on with your life. Of course, never admit the source of your guilt to anyone else.

TIP:
Stop trying to remove guilt from your life and you'll have a lot more free time.

I'll tell your BOYFRIEND
You ONCE BOUGHT A
BARRY MANILOW RECORD
AND YOUR NICKNAME WAS
MANGO.

threats

THREATS

When you have an argument and it's not going your way, it is time to bring out the threats. Not serious threats that make a person fear for his welfare but mild threats that expose the hypocrisy of your opponent and leave him vulnerable.

Some threats are the tattletale type: I'll tell your parents that we really don't leave town at Christmastime, I'll tell the kids that you did it at their age and they are the result, I'll tell your boss that you really don't have a degree in urban planning. The best threats to use at your place of employment generally involve the telephone: I'll call the Health Department, I'll call the IRS, I'll call Immigration. Soon you'll be working your own hours with a nice big raise.

TIP:

When you feel like the sparkle has gone out of your relationship, an occasional lighthearted threat will certainly turn up the passion.

I'd love to give him my opinion but he might be someone to suck up to.

OPINIONS COUNT

If you long to be sought out for your understanding on any matter (regardless of whether you have any knowledge of the subject), then you need to have an opinion on everything. Your opinion doesn't necessarily have to reflect your true feelings. What counts is having an opinion.

An opinion can be formed with long thoughtful contemplation—"The reason why the economy is dead can be traced back to the decline of the railroad"—or with quick, spur-of-the-moment observations—"I've thought about it for days and I just can't stand Jenny's haircut or the way she treats her plants." The trick is to have an opinion ready for any occasion.

As you practice voicing your opinion you will notice that changes in your delivery can make a world of difference and influence the decisions of others. You may find that you wish to give a scathing opinion about someone you despise, or you may want to simply observe that you could care less about that person and her measly life. This position actually puts her down even more while elevating your status in the process.

TIP:

The only time not to have an opinion is when you need to suck up to someone.

JADED PHRASES

Oh, really.
I've seen it before.
Who cares. yawn.
DOESN'T IMPRESS ME
for A SECOND. No, I
DIDN'T NOTICE. It
DOESN'T MATTER.

ACTING JADED

Acting jaded is the cultured person's way of meditating. It is the perfect relaxation exercise to fit our stressed-out lives. For full benefit, merely turn the head slowly from shoulder to shoulder, eyeing the room with no particular interest. There should never be any eye contact made. Everything should seem so dreadfully commonplace.

Being jaded is an attitude of composure, maturity and worldliness. Not showing much concern for the newest person at work will make you seem jaded. No facial expression except for a pained grimace at the mention of the latest trend gives you the air of being jaded. To be jaded means to yawn and always be on the verge of being bored stiff while everyone is bowing, pouring compliments over you and being in an ecstatic state.

The following are some posing tips for jaded people: Wear pale blues, grays and whites—you may go to lilac, damask blue or periwinkle. Never drink well liquor; instead, drink name brands, and always clear liquor. Your cigarette is held rather than smoked.

Tip:
Do not go as far as being aloof. You can still be friendly and polite while being jaded.

Make Them get on their knees— then *don't* forgive them.

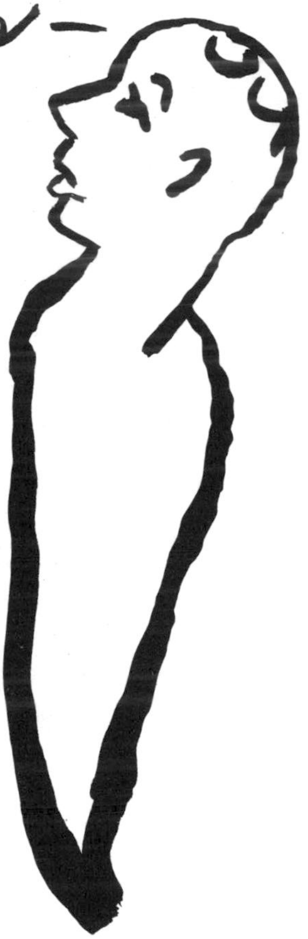

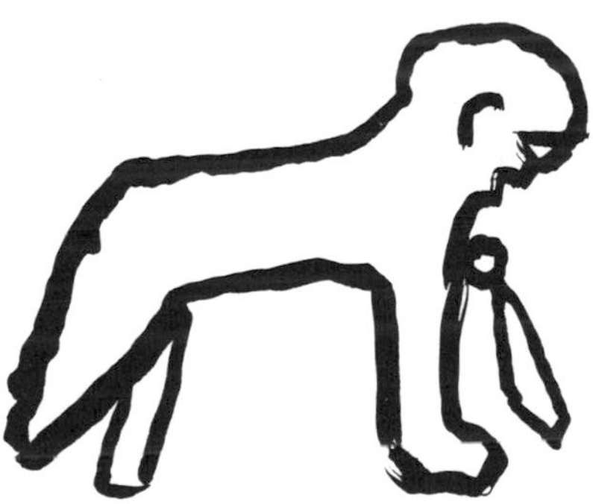

FORGIVING IS FOR SUCKERS

If someone does something bad to you, why the hell should you forgive him? Stop going over and over the bad event with the idea that if you can forgive the perpetrator you will be relieved of the pain, the memory or the trauma. Forgiving is saying that you understand why someone hurt you. Forgiving is for suckers.

I say hold a grudge. A grudge is a fuel that can be used to accomplish things. Whenever I hear a victim say he has forgiven someone it makes me sick. Once we forgive we are considered a softy. Let everyone know that you hold a grudge and people will know that you are strong.

Everyone wants to be forgiven and given a second chance—forget it. The forgiveness routine was invented to make us think that there is something wrong with us until we forgive and forget. Remember, there is nothing wrong with you that holding a grudge won't take care of.

REMEMBER:
Momentary forgiveness is all right if it guarantees an expensive gift.

BEING THE CENTER
OF ATTENTION
DOES WONDERS
FOR THE
COMPLEXION

SELF-CENTERING

We all must learn the art of changing the subject to focus on the subject of ourselves. This means directing all conversation back to you.

One good way is just to say I, I, I and me, me, me in regard to everything and to wear wrist jewelry, scarves and flowing sleeves to move around in and draw attention to yourself as you change the subject. Act as if the subject you are interrupting and changing is tired and dreadful, while you are fascinating and absorbing.

Announce the interruption; for example in discussions ranging from economics to the final episode of *Gilligan's Island*, say, "I want a drink," or "I slept with someone named Ginger." Of course, everyone is interested in sex, so then you can direct the attention to yourself and command the entire conversation to revolve around you.

MOTTO:

Everything is always more pleasant when we are the center of attention.

ABOUT THE AUTHOR

Karen Finley was born in Chicago, received a Master of Fine Arts degree from the San Francisco Art Institute and currently lives outside of New York City. She is a visual and performance artist and also writes and directs plays, records albums, appears in films and has authored a book, *Shock Treatment* (City Lights Books, 1990). She has had numerous installations and exhibitions of her drawings and presentations of her performances throughout North America and Europe.